CORRIS
NOSTALGIA

Brynedwin Stores, Corris, *c*.1951, colloquially known as 'Shop Parsons' during this period when it was one of the main focal points of the village. It lay across the road from the Institute, was adjacent to the Post Office and well-placed for bus stops for Tywyn, Dolgellau, Machynlleth and Aberllefenni. 1951.

GBJ

CORRIS
NOSTALGIA

Gwyn Briwnant Jones

Gomer

Published in 2015 by
Gomer Press, Llandysul, Ceredigion SA44 4JL
www.gomer.co.uk

ISBN 978 1 78562 075 1

A CIP record for this title is available from the British Library.

Printed and bound in Wales at
Gomer Press, Llandysul, Ceredigion

Contents

A village in the Cader Idris country.
Corris, on the G.W.R. Road Motor Service from Machynlleth or Dolgelley.

The expansion of GW bus services in central Wales during the 1920s and '30s provided much extra work for the railway's photographic and publicity departments. This unhackneyed view of Corris was one result of these endeavours; it was used as a frontispiece in the *GW Magazine* for July 1930, and serves the same purpose again in 2015, 85 years later. Undated.   *GW Official.*

Acknowledgements

My grateful thanks are offered to Richard Saffery for drafting the Foreword, and equally grateful appreciation is extended to other members of the Corris Railway Society, particularly Alf Oxford, Richard Greenhough, David and Meinir Coleman, and Richard Kidner. Others who have helped generously with various photographic matters were Alan Jarvis; P. Q. Treloar; G. H. Platt; W. G. Rear; and The Great Western Trust, Didcot, particularly Philip Kelley and John Cummings but also The Kidderminster Railway Museum; Don Newey, Archivist of the Tal-y-llyn Railway Museum, Tywyn; R. S. Carpenter, Photographs; Mrs Joan Brame, Machynlleth; Huw Lewis, Aberdyfi; Chris Taylor, Cardiff; Glyn Williams, Meifod; Peter Mitchell, Cardiff; the National Railway Museum and the Omnibus Society.

Finally, my most grateful thanks are extended to the efficient and friendly workforce at Gomer Press who, together with Dr Dyfed Elis-Gruffydd have consistently maintained the highest professional standards over many years.

It has been a pleasure to work with them.

Gwyn Briwnant Jones
Cardiff, 2015

This large card displayed comprehensive information in various ticket outlets throughout the region. The reverse side carried well-known local views, including a photograph of a new charabanc, (p. 24); all by D. S. George & Son.

GBJ Coll.

Foreword

It is a privilege to write the foreword to another of Gwyn Briwnant-Jones' seminal collections of anecdotes and facts about the local 'family affair' that was the 'Old Corris'.

These gems are lovingly recalled and clearly relayed for the benefit of current and future generations of Corrisites. He continues to enhance our view of the historic railway through vitalising detail of its place in the industrial and communal life of the area that it served. If there is to be a fuller understanding of its history, it is essential to record and pass on these ever-receding 'remembrances' of activities on and around the railway. This record perfectly complements the photographs that so many enthusiasts will scrutinize, if only to continue their love affair with the line.

Gwyn's warm and wise support and encouragement to the pioneers who started the Corris Railway's unlikely revival, and to those who continue to apply their tenacity and skills to the challenges of safely running, maintaining and extending it, are greatly indebted to him for so generously giving his time to research thoroughly and then to present beautifully so much of the life and soul of the 'Old Corris'. His personal knowledge and experience of the railway fully qualify him in turn to be part of its ever-growing heritage.

Richard Saffery
Member
Corris Railway Society

CORRIS RAILWAY

ROAD

Motor Services

BETWEEN

Machynlleth, Aberdovey & Towyn,

(WEEK DAYS ONLY)

COMMENCING FEBRUARY 4th.

TIME TABLE. To Aberdovey and Towyn.

			a.m.	a.m.		p.m.	p.m.	p.m.
MACHYNLLETH (Clock Tower)	dep		8 0	9 0	12 0		3 0	4 0
HAFODTY	dep		8 7	9 7	12 7		3 7	4 7
TAINEWYDDION			8 16	9 16	12 16		3 16	4 16
PENNAL			8 20	9 20	12 20		3 20	4 20
GOGARTH			8 34	9 34	12 34		3 34	4 34
TAFOLGRAIG			8 42	9 42	12 42		3 42	4 42
TREFRI FAWR			8 48	9 48	12 48		3 48	4 48
ABERDOVEY (Harbour)			9 0	9 55	12 55		3 55	4 55
TREFEDDIAN TERRACE			9 3	10 3	1 3		4 3	5 3
OLD MILL			9 10	10 10	1 10		4 10	5 10
TOWYN (Corbett Arms)	arr.		9 18	10 18	1 18		4 18	5 18

To Aberdovey and Machynlleth.

		a.m.	p.m.	p.m.	p.m.
TOWYN (Corbett Arms)	dep	10 30	1 30	4 30	7 30
OLD MILL		10 38	1 38	4 38	7 38
TREFEDDIAN TERRACE		10 45	1 45	4 45	7 45
ABERDOVEY (Harbour)		10 55	1 55	4 55	7 55
TREFRI FAWR		11 0	2 0	5 0	8 0
TAFOLGRAIG		11 8	2 8	5 8	8 8
GOGARTH		11 14	2 14	5 14	8 14
PENNAL		11 28	2 28	5 28	8 28
TAINEWYDDION		11 32	2 32	5 32	8 32
HAFODTY		11 41	2 41	5 41	8 41
MACHYNLLETH (Clock Tower)		11 48	2 48	5 48	8 48

SINGLE FARES.

STAGE NUMBER.		1	2	3	4	5	6	7	8	9	10
STAGE		Machynlleth (Clock Tower)	Hafodty	Tainewyddion	Pennal	Gogarth	Tafolgraig	Trefri Fawr	Aberdovey (Harbour)	Trefeddian Ter. & Cwm Saru	Old Mill
		s. d.	s. d.	s. d.	s. d.	s. d.	s. d.	s. d.	s. d.	s. d.	s. d.
HAFODTY		0 2									
TAINEWYDDION		0 40	2								
PENNAL		0 60	40	40							
GOGARTH		0 80	60	40	2						
TAFOLGRAIG (For Happy Valley)		0 100	60	60	40	2					
TREFRI FAWR		1 00	100	80	60	40	2				
ABERDOVEY (Harbour)		1 00	100	80	60	40	2				
TREFEDDIAN TER. & Cwm Safo		1 41	21	00	100	80	60	40	2		
OLD MILL (For Happy Valley)		1 71	51	31	10	110	90	70	50	A	
TOWYN (Corbett Arms)		1 91	71	51	31	10	110	90	70	50	

Minimum fare 2d. Children over 3 and under 12 carried at half fares to nearest penny.
For general notices & regulations relating to the Company's Motor Services and for particulars as
Private Hire, apply General Manager, Machynlleth

Machynlleth, Feb. 1924.

D. J. McCOURT, *General Manager.*

J. Evans, Printer, Machynlleth.

John Evans, a Machynlleth printer, was given regular commissions by the Corris company; this flyer is an example, which was produced for the new bus service to Towyn [*sic*], inaugurated on 4 February 1924.

GBJ Coll.

Preface

Any who witnessed the demise of the old Corris Railway in 1948 can surely recall the feeling of gloom and sadness at that time. There was then, obviously, no way of anticipating a revival of the railway, in any form, but subsequent events have been little short of miraculous. Thanks to the enthusiasm, dedication and sheer hard work by members, the railway has a bright future before it once more.

Publication of *A Corris Celebration* in 2009 was intended as this writer's final account of the Corris Railway, but as has happened occasionally during recent years, various photographs or artefacts have emerged unexpectedly to stir the memory and kindle fresh impetus for another slim publication – as good a means as most, of safeguarding photographs and printed material and making them accessible to the growing band of Corris aficionados. Hopefully, this final reflective glance at the past will be acceptable, midst all the excitement and clamour of new works.

Time, however, has reduced the store of memories of the old line, requiring a conscious effort to avoid too much obvious repetition; understandably also, the number of new photographs to be included is much less. Consequently, acceptable standards have had to be modified in a few instances but one or two prints and hopefully a few of the printed artefacts can compensate here, for they will be 'new' to most readers. Would that there were more of their kind, but their store is also finite and only very few can now remain to be discovered. We must be grateful for what has survived.

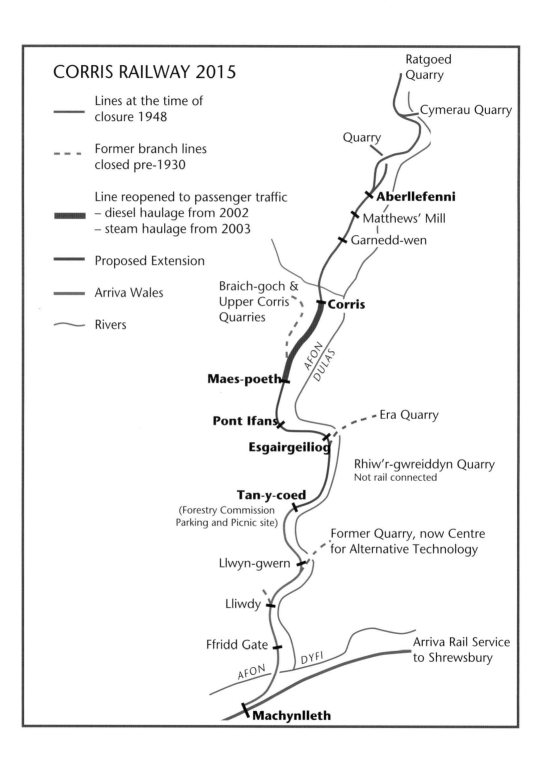

CORRIS RAILWAY 2015

Lines at the time of
closure 1948

Former branch lines
closed pre-1930

Line reopened to passenger traffic
– diesel haulage from 2002
– steam haulage from 2003

Proposed Extension

Arriva Wales

Rivers

Ratgoed
Quarry

Cymerau Quarry

Quarry

Aberllefenni

Matthews' Mill

Garnedd-wen

Braich-goch &
Upper Corris
Quarries

Corris

AFON
DULAS

Maes-poeth

Pont Ifans

Era Quarry

Esgairgeiliog

Rhiw'r-gwreiddyn Quarry
Not rail connected

Tan-y-coed

(Forestry Commission
Parking and Picnic site)

Former Quarry, now Centre
for Alternative Technology

Llwyn-gwern

Lliwdy

Ffridd Gate

DYFI

Arriva Rail Service
to Shrewsbury

AFON

Machynlleth

1. MEMORIES
1938–1948

A few aspects of the last years of the old Corris Railway – incorporating one or two events which pre-date the final decade – somehow, still survive in the memory. Rather surprisingly, perhaps, these include two road improvement schemes in the Machynlleth area. Obviously alien in a railway context, they serve to pinpoint other important events within that era and feature two sites, either side of Dyfi Bridge, where a combination of narrow carriageways and severe bends were eased in late 1936 and early 1937; they became exciting locations for a youngster with a normal interest in transport matters.

Funfairs and circuses in the field alongside the Corris Railway at Machynlleth, were a fairly common sight before and just after the last war, but one which rarely attracted special attention. After Sir Robert Fossett's visit in 1958, circuses came no more and visiting funfairs were re-located near the centre of the town. This view captures well the spirit of that pre-war era. *c.*1937.

A. E. Rimmer.

The work was instigated by the impending approach of the Royal National Eisteddfod of Wales to Machynlleth, between the 2nd and 7th August, 1937. This extremely popular annual event attracts a multitude of visitors from all parts of the country each year, wherever it is held. In addition to special trains which transported thousands of main line passengers during eisteddfod week, particular efforts were made that year to improve two of the more hazardous sections of road at the approach to the town, notably below the Ffridd on the Corris road and below Penrhyn Dyfi, on the Aberdyfi road. Only in later years did the full realization dawn that this may well have been one of the last occasions for the employment of horses and carts, and hot tar and chippings, on road-building in the locality. It was virtually the end of an era for such antiquated methods.

The end of another era was also approaching on the nearby Corris Railway. Even when taken over by the Great Western in 1930, the Corris was hardly in the rudest of health; eight years later, its decline was much more obvious. Just a few solitary features remained as reminders of the comparative affluence of earlier times. The run-around loop at Machynlleth, for example, used during passenger days, still survived, although textured by the deep red rust of almost a decade of inactivity and neglect. Tall grasses and young shrubs grew unhindered between the sleepers, together with the dreaded Japanese knotweed, which was already colonising at the western end of the loop. It flourished and in next to no time had spread over an area five or six times the original outbreak.

Hugh B. Tours' general view looking toward the end of the line at Machynlleth. The major change at this point after the end of passenger services, concerned the demolition of the former carriage shed/bus garage (left) and eventual removal of the loop-line, on the right. 31 May 1936.

Hugh B. Tours

This redundant signalling frame, amidst the brambles near the narrow-gauge weigh-table at Machynlleth, failed to escape the attention of the scrap merchant in 1940/1. 12 August 1935.

H. F. Wheeler,
courtesy of R. S. Carpenter.

Although not of the Corris era, this view from the rock is included as it records the location of the Corris signal-box, when removed to the upper yard *c*.1941. Its roof is visible opposite the open door of the right-hand van of the pair in the end loading-bay. The Corris station building and former bus garage in the lower yard remain intact but the old iron mink body used as a loco coal store has disappeared. The two modest concrete buildings on the old Braich-goch wharf served as a temporary store during rebuilding of the main-line goods warehouse, commenced in 1960. As the photograph was being taken, an unidentified Manor (very possibly No. 7818) ran in with the down *Cambrian Coast Express*. *c*.1962.

Kidderminster Railway Museum.

Yet, in 1938, the loop's sleepers and rails could still be seen, apparently just awaiting the progress of a locomotive to annihilate the invasive foliage and grind away some of the deep-seated rust, to re-establish the old order. But this was day-dreaming, mere wishful thinking. Within little more than a year, the country was at war and the nationwide drive for scrap metal ensured that any iron or steel not gainfully employed would be rapidly committed to the furnaces; the old passenger loop was an obvious target. What had hitherto survived of the Corris's signalling system was also promptly dispatched, when all surviving signals, together with the boxes at Machynlleth, Maes-poeth and Corris, quickly disappeared. The box which controlled the loop and cross-over, alongside the former carriage shed/bus garage at Machynlleth, was an early candidate for demolition, principally because the floorboards had decayed, having been built at ground level and apparently without an effective damp-proof course. Machynlleth's second box, to the east, slightly larger and constructed on a raised slate base, was clear of the ground and flood water; consequently, its better condition ensured that the GWR found further use for it. Around 1941, it was dismantled and removed to the upper yard, where it joined the Signal & Telegraph Department's collection of assorted stores and cabins. It survived well into the mid-1960s and saw out the age of steam on the Cambrian.

As the frames of the old signal-boxes were removed, their control was governed by newly-installed ground levers. These were padlocked when introduced but the practice did not last long. Towards the end of this period of regression, a slight but pronounced growth in traffic became noticeable, largely as a result of repairs to bomb-damage in London and elsewhere. Pre-war train loads on the Corris, which, during the 1930s, usually averaged between 4 and 6 waggons daily, increased quite noticeably to between 10 and 12. On several occasions loads up to 14 were observed, which created quite an impressive train when viewed through the end window of Price Owen's van.

The mini-boom, however, did not endure, for within a year or so, the demand had fallen away markedly. This seemed to coincide with a period of increased restraint and restrictions; the period when rationing of most commodities became much more apparent and when constant efforts were made to economize further. The Corris played its part, as services were reduced to run on alternate days.

Thereafter, the gradual decline continued, becoming more apparent with each season. Yet, even without a passenger service, without any signalling and deprived of the staff of yesteryear, the Corris continued to operate and managed to attract the attention of discerning enthusiasts. Even though the passenger service had ceased, a steady number of visitors continued to be drawn to the 'lein-fach', the little line. Occasionally, some even arrived at the station armed with official passes, but these were in the minority; most were opportunists who were content to take a chance and just turn up – they seemed invariably to be lucky. The little train, however, was quite capable of attracting random passengers *en route* and seemed to specialize in picking-up weary hikers or sodden cyclists. Rarely was anyone refused a lift.

The first of three views of No. 4 – to reflect its more intensive use during the early 1940s, after return from an intermediate repair at Swindon in September 1940. With Driver Humphreys, outside Maes-poeth shed on 13 June 1942.

Kidderminster Railway Museum.

No. 4 about to leave Machynlleth for Corris and Aberllefenni, with a load of coal. 11 April 1947.

GBJ

Inside Maes-poeth, 20 July 1947. No. 4 was in regular use at this time but by 9 December 1947 it was 'stopped' until 21 January 1948. Its reprieve, however, was short-lived; it was stopped finally, on 6 May 1948.

Kidderminster Railway Museum.

This is not to say that such travellers were always in evidence – that would not be accurate – but there was undoubtedly a relaxed attitude amongst the staff toward casual passengers, a factor also noted by others. Obviously, no records were kept of numbers, nor regrettably, was there any form of 'Visitor's Book' but amongst those who paid the Corris a visit were several prominent members of the narrow-gauge fraternity, including Roger Kidner, Hugh B. Tours, W. E. Hayward, Selwyn H. P. Higgins, J. I. C. Boyd and Lewis Cozens. The appeal of the Corris may be epitomized by a footnote on a postcard from Hayward in 1962, twenty-one years after his visit: 'except that it was during that terrible War period one would like to go back again to 1941 and riding up again to Corris with Humphreys and Owen'.

The writer's personal trips along the line were always memorable and a source of great joy. Those early journeys were with Price Owen in the guard's van, which invariably seemed to be well-laden. The long hinged bench, opposite the sliding door, was usually 'down', with

No. 3 was then brought into use for the final months of operation, during which time the locomotives were stabled behind the station building at Machynlleth. The Falcon is portrayed here with five drams of slates at Aberllefenni, at the furthermost point for locomotive operation from Machynlleth. The slates would have been brought to this location by Dafydd Roberts and the GW horse. 9 July 1948.

GBJ

This popular photograph is used once more as it illustrates so well Price Owen's mishap with the stove. The van displayed the pink primer for only a brief period, but was well-recorded for posterity in this anonymous photograph. *c*.1947.

Real Photographs.

the space beneath occupied by what appeared to be a tangle of assorted loose couplings, ropes and tarpaulins. The latter, as were discovered years later, were dedicated to the Corris. The GWR Service Appendix, for March 1943, noted: 'The sheets for use on this branch must not under any consideration be sent or used beyond Machynlleth'. The loose couplings were used by the guard to replace some of the primitive examples used on the quarry stock; these had a habit of springing out of their 'seating' during a journey, much to the consternation of the staff. The replacement shackles were useful accessories and were always husbanded most jealously and collected fastidiously by the guard at the end of each journey.

It was remarkable what might be found shoe-horned into the van; the variety of merchandise was fascinating with any bulky items or 'overflow' found in open waggons, protected by tarpaulin in wet weather. Within, besides an array of parcels of different shapes and sizes, might be found some interesting 'branded' goods – cases of Lyons Cakes were favourites, for Parsons or Jarvis Stores in Corris, or a box labelled to a private address, from J. D. Williams of Manchester – favoured as a Ladies Outfitter throughout north Wales at that time. Pet rabbits in cages or a box or two of live chicks could also be found among the assorted traffic on occasion … or perhaps an item of Lugage in Advance. This was not as unusual as might be supposed for, even without an official passenger service, inhabitants of the Dulas valley bound to or from the main line made full use of the Corris in those days. On one particular occasion, a suitcase was noted, covered carefully with stout brown paper and securely tied with strong string – no selotape or brown parcel tape in those days. Judging by the pristine condition of the leather handle, which protruded from the brown paper, it was easy to imagine that the owner had recently invested in a new leather case and had no wish to see it scuffed in transit!

On Tuesdays, the van would be kept as clear as possible, for the Machynlleth Station Master made his weekly inspection of the branch that day. This was regarded as an essential duty, and though not a particularly onerous one, there was little in the way of comfort in the van. Consequently, particularly in later years, it was known for a sturdy Captain's Chair to be brought down from the High Level station and installed midst the parcels. During cold weather the small iron stove, located in the left-hand corner, provided enough warmth to appease the guard on his constant forays into and out of the cold. The coal came from the locomotive's stock. During the spell of severe winter weather in 1947, the fire in the little stove was stoked up so enthusiastically by Price Owen that it became red hot and set the woodwork alight! Fortunately, this was controlled before too much damage was done, but the van still had to be withdrawn to spend a few days in Maes-poeth under repair. The new wood – after a short period in a pink primer – appeared in a dark shade of chocolate, whilst the rest of the van remained weather-beaten GW grey.

In common with the rest of the country, the war years saw increased employment of women in a variety of occupations. The Corris was no exception and made its own modest contribution.

Miss Lizzie Humphreys ran the small office at Corris station, collecting parcels for dispatch or distributing consignments which had arrived by rail. A small sack-truck was used around the village, emblazoned with 'Corris' and the 'Tare' weight on one of the shafts. Larger items – furniture frequently – were dealt with by Dafydd Roberts and the horse and cart, who operated as far afield as Upper Corris, Esgairgeiliog and Aberllefenni. Although stabled in Corris, where railway horses had been stabled since the opening of the railway, the GW horse was also responsible for shunting slate and slab waggons at Aberllefenni and for operating the Ratgoed/Cymerau traffic.

Invitations from Humphrey to travel on the footplate became more numerous during the final years, from about 1946. During the early part of this period, No.4 was usually the duty engine. No. 3 only ventured out on those rare occasions when the rails were dry, or when the Kerr Stuart required some minor attention; a state of affairs which continued until May 1947, when No. 4 was 'stopped' by a defective boiler/firebox. No. 3 was then called upon to continue alone, until closure in August 1948. As most of the writer's footplate journeys occurred in 1947/8, the majority were therefore on board No. 3 and usually entailed sitting out-of-the-way, on top of the coal; a small price to pay for an otherwise enchanting experience.

After the operation of the last train on 20 August 1948, the rolling stock remained discretely obscured behind the station in Machynlleth until it was sent by rail, to Tywyn, in March 1951. 13 September 1949.

R. S. Carpenter Photos.

The final form of the old station at Corris. The small booking-office window set into the wall was still apparent even at this late date, although it had not been used for over a quarter of a century. August 1956.

Kidderminster Railway Museum.

A fresh begining. The Corris Society was just too late to save the station building at Corris, but grasped the opportunity to save the old stables and coach-house, which have since been very successfully adapted as a small museum and refreshment room. Plans are being developed to improve the track layout. 22 April 1969.

R. F. Roberts/The Stephenson Locomotive Society

By the late 1940s, loads were much reduced and could at best only be described as modest, possibly half-a-dozen waggons at most, whereas all too often during this period, there were perhaps just two or three. Contrary to expectations, coal traffic was more prominent during the summer months, as the prudent took advantage of discounted prices to stock-up before winter set in. This traffic was actually more predictable than that emanating from the quarries, which were often beset by irregular production or strikes at this time, although the order books were healthy.

So the Corris approached its end. Even the optimistic had to acknowledge that the old line was tired and worn. There were no bells to sound a death knell, no wreath to signify the last journey, only the river quietly eroding the bank up-stream of the bridge, providing a silent, irreversible indication that there would be no reprieve, no escape. No longer a case of 'if', it had become a matter of 'when'. Another heavy flood over the weekend of 21-22 August, precipitated an urgent inspection of the line at the first opportunity, probably either late on Sunday or early on Monday. But the last train had already run on Friday, 20 August. Further details of the closure have been noted previously, in *Great Western Corris*, together with information regarding the transfer of stock to Tywyn, for use on the Tal-y-llyn Railway.

Thus the Corris expired after 89 years, without any hope of rescue ... until the formation of the Corris Railway Society in 1966.

Those wishing to learn more of the Society's achievements and latest plans, together with membership details, are invited to contact the membership secretary:

John Rudkin
2 Roseberry Court
Tockett's Mill
Guisborough
TS14 6QA

An A5 SAE would be appreciated,

2. CORRIS BUSES

The Corris, alone amongst the Welsh narrow-gauge companies, could boast of operating its own road services. These had evolved from an early desire to extend the railway's appeal beyond mere local needs, in order to cater also for the burgeoning tourist industry. From as early as the 1880s, the enchantment of the narrow-gauge had served to attract new tourists to Corris – what could be more natural than to extend that appeal to encompass Tal-y-llyn and Cadair Idris? This was initially achieved by means of horse-drawn wagonettes, from what became an interchange point at Corris. This proved most advantageous, for it emphasised a contrast between the smooth-running and novel *bijou* saloons of the narrow-gauge from Machynlleth – which provided kaleidoscopic views of the charming Dulas valley – and the altogether more rugged transportation provided by the horse-drawn carriages which introduced the travellers to the romantic terrain *en route* to the lake. Between them, the two sections proved most agreeable and contributed to an entertaining excursion which was popular and successful for over forty years.

When the development of the internal combustion engine brought dramatic improvements in the new century, J. J. O'Sullivan, then Corris manager, appealed to

From the earliest days of the 1880s, horses supplied the means by which the growing number of tourists sampled the more difficult regions of Wales. Indeed, one wonders at their power, not only to haul, but also to brake. What, precisely, might a Health and Safety executive make of this horse-drawn carriage and at least sixteen passengers, having safely reached the valley floor after negotiating some steep gradients on its way from Corris? *c.*1900.

George's Series V & S Ltd.

Matters changed dramatically from 1910 onwards as motor charabancs were introduced. To advertise these and their services, the railway produced flyers, posters and large cards with illustrations of the charabancs, their fares and their timings. This illustration is taken from such a card (p. 8), which has survived the intervening century in remarkably fine condition. 1914.

GBJ Coll.

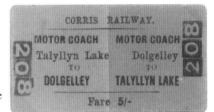

An undated return ticket from Dolgellau to Tal-y-llyn Lake. The 5/- fare could hardly be regarded as cheap.

Another view of one of the new charabancs about to set out from Corris to Tal-y-llyn. The driver is Edward Pattison, whose father had been an engine driver on the Corris and, previously, on the Tal-y-llyn Railway also. William Morris, the Station Master, is the shorter figure on the right, wearing a railway cap. AE 3184 was first registered in 1916.

Private Collection.

his Bristol HQ to purchase or hire one of the new motor charabancs then begining to appear in the area, but apparently, not one was available in 1907. However, preparations were made for the inevitable, and later, in 1908, Mr R. Jones Pritchard – one of the regular carriage drivers – was sent to Bristol for retraining as a charabanc driver and to gain his driving licence. Eventually, two new 20-seat vehicles, finished in the blue livery of the Bristol Tramway & Carriage Company were hired and, from 8 July 1911, they operated very successfully between Dolgellau, Corris and Tal-y-llyn, and drew favourable comments from the *Aberystwyth Observer.* At the end of the season, both returned to Bristol to 'winter', accompanied by a request for an increase in their number the following season. In 1912, three duly arrived, and were based at Dolgellau and Aberystwyth; two remained in the area over the winter whilst the third returned to Bristol. By 1913, five charabancs were operating from Aberystwyth, Corris, Dolgellau and Machynlleth, and the following year, a Circular Tour was introduced, the first of several different routes which emerged over the years.

This is a rare close-up of a Burford with its driver, J. W. Evans, universally and popularly known as 'Jack Tal-y-bont'. The buses were initially run from the Corris station at Machynlleth. The solid rubber tyre and metal wheel are immediately noticeable, as is the driver's leather uniform, leggings and Bell Punch – which are most impressive.

Courtesy Mrs Joan Brame.

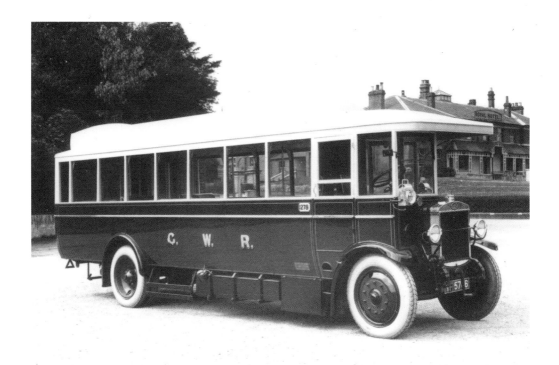

This remarkable photograph is of the very bus – Guy FBB, GW No. YF 1278, reg. no. 5746 – which was dispatched when new in 1927 to Glandyfi station, then acting as the depot for the Machynlleth–Aberystwyth service. It operated from Glandyfi/Machynlleth, until at least 1930.

Great Western Trust, Didcot.

The period immediately following the First World War saw a rapid growth of road services throughout the country, stimulated by the large number of men trained as drivers during the war, and by the ready availability of ex-Army vehicles which flooded the market at this time. Furthermore, there was little in the way of strict control and regulations. With no shortage of viable schemes and hindered by confusion, the Aberystwyth Town Council found itself at the centre of a licensing controversy, which appeared to favour some applicants at the expense of others.

In 1923, for example, the Corris and Crosville companies applied to Aberystwyth Council for licences to operate services from Machynlleth to Aberystwyth (also to Tywyn and Devil's Bridge), but permission was withheld as the council delayed their decision to allow the Great Western time to apply for a licence of their own. This was duly granted and the Great Western launched their Aberystwyth–Machynlleth service on 29 November 1923.

Understandably, both the Corris and Crosville were displeased with this arrangement and appealed to the Minister of Transport, resulting eventually in a meeting with the Great Western on 15 April 1924. The outcome sanctioned the Great Western and Corris companies to work the Aberystwyth route (excluding Crosville). The Devil's Bridge route was then operated by Crosville and Corris (excluding the Great Western); Crosville was granted the Ysbyty Ystwyth route and the Great Western was awarded the Cardigan route. The early 1920s would appear to have been tempestuous years for bus operators in central Wales.

As no convenient site for a garage could be found at either Aberystwyth or Machynlleth, the buses on this route worked out of Glandyfi station yard, located conveniently on the main Machynlleth–Aberystwyth road, the Grouping of 1923 having recently brought this former Cambrian property into the Great Western fold. Local crews operated the services which, from 1924, were worked by AEC and Burford vehicles, but in May 1927, a brand-new Guy FBB No. 1278, registration number YF 5746 was stationed there; it stayed at least until 1930. Most interestingly, a sister vehicle, Guy FBB No. 1268, has been saved from destruction and in recent years impeccably and painstakingly restored. It is periodically 'exercised' in the Thames Valley area.

The next generation of buses to appear in Corris included the popular Burfords, which emerged in the early 1920s and used on services from Machynlleth to Newtown; one is seen here calling at the Wynnstay Arms, Llanbryn-mair. They also appeared on Aberllefenni, Aberhosan, Tywyn and Dinas Mawddwy services. *c*.1925.

GBJ Coll.

Meanwhile, although its rail services were weakening during this decade, the Corris concentrated on opening further bus routes. In 1924, these ran to Tywyn, Dinas Mawddwy, Newtown (Tuesdays only) and Aberhosan (Wednesdays and Stock Sale days only). There was also, for a brief period, a direct Dolgellau–Machynlleth service, before this reverted to an older pattern of Machynlleth–Aberllefenni services, following the railway route. This later connected with services from Tywyn and Dolgellau, meeting in the station yard at Corris. When the three services met here, twice a day, in very restricted circumstances, the congestion was considerable. Before 1930, space was also required by passenger trains. Furthermore, in order to achieve this rendezvous, the Tywyn and Dolgellau buses, had to negotiate a ferocious hairpin bend near the Braich Goch Hotel in Corris, which required patient and skillful 'shunting' across the main road, four times a day. The practice dated from the earliest days of horse-drawn carriages and continued through to c.1975.

The driver of a Crosville Leyland Cub (N101) reveals the limited space available for negotiating the turn into and out of Corris village. Matters became more difficult over the years, as the buses grew in length. They continued to turn here, up till about 1975; by that time they had increased in length to 36 ft.

Omnibus Society.

A view by the official Great Western photographer, dated July 1928, initially to illustrate the incursion by GW bus services into the mid-Wales area, also serves to reveal one or two other interesting features. Firstly, it shows that the Upper Corris branch line, although believed to have been lightly laid with bridge rails, appears nonetheless to have been very well-constructed. Secondly, the photographer's elevated position demonstrates clearly the severity of the hairpin bend which had to be negotiated each time a Dolgellau or Tywyn bus entered and left the village. The challenge was first encountered by the horse-drawn carriages of the 1880s and, thereafter, by a succession of bus drivers, for almost a century. Here, Fleet No. 883, Burford ND Forward Control 30 cwt chassis (with Buckingham body), pauses before turning down to Corris, on a service from Machynlleth.

GW Official.

When the GW decided to withdraw the narrow-gauge passenger services, from the end of 1930, the buses were transferred to the Wrexham and District Omnibus Company, which was quickly renamed the Western Transport Omnibus Company. Within a very brief period, this was duly taken over by Crosville who, from 1 May 1933, promptly set about providing improved facilities at Machynlleth, opening a new garage there in 1935 on a site which straddled the route of the erstwhile horse-tramway to Derwen-las.

Despite being seen by many as the enemy of the little train, the Crosville proved fascinating for local bus enthusiasts, particularly during the 1940s, when around half-a-dozen buses were garaged there. From the late 1930s, Crosville had introduced a bus numbering system which divided the various types into 'classes' and gave bus-spotting added interest. Coaches, for example, were prefixed 'K' and numbered accordingly – K47 being a favourite which divided its time between Machynlleth and Aberystwyth. The 'K's were petrol engined, as were the remainder of the allocation at that time, including the little

A Corris Railway bus on a Bristol 4-ton chassis, under repair at Machynlleth, *c.*1934.

Modern Transport.

A 'soft' print, but a great survivor, taken in the station yard at Machynlleth. Left to right: Charlie Evans, carpenter; Robert Ieuan Roberts, apprentice; Will Owen, apprentice (later landlord of the Eagles Hotel) and Trevor Griffiths, engineman. This bus featured in a previous photograph of the Newtown service at Llanbryn-mair, but appears by this time to sport pneumatic tyres. *c.*1929.

Corris Railway Society.

No one quite knows why this early Clement Bayard was on the books of the Corris Railway, perhaps for private hire or for occasional use by railway heirarchy, but when the GWR took over in 1930 it was promptly ordered back to Bristol. A letter despatched to Bristol from the General Manager's Office at Machynlleth on 20 August 1930, stated: 'Six of our omnibuses here left today for Bristol by road'. (Registration numbers FF 1445, TA 8114, TA 8115, TA 8116, TA 8118 and HU 6128.)

'The four-seater Clement Bayard AE 2246 [*above*] has been forwarded today to Bristol by rail: Austin car EP 3932 has been forwarded by rail to Paddington and the ten-seater Clement Bayard AE 3177 is still here.'

It seems likely that when the order came to return Clement Bayard AE 2246 to Bristol, the opportunity was taken in Corris to celebrate with a light-hearted, unofficial group photograph.

NRM Selwyn Pearce Higgins Collection.

bus then associated most fondly with the Corris route, a Leyland Cub, N72. Even though this was when most buses were normally crewed by a conductor as well as a driver, certain lightly-laden routes, such as the services to Aberhosan, Tal-y-wern, or the early morning Aberllefenni service, were covered by a Cub. This little 'one-man' bus boasted a fascinating modification to the folding entry door – a sort of extended chromium-plated loop-handle, which enabled the driver to reach across and operate the door without needing to leave his seat. Nowadays, of course, all would be achieved at the touch of a button.

Later on during the war, the loading on the Corris route proved too much for the Cubs, which were replaced by Leyland 'Lions' B42, B43 and B55. Even so, the Aberllefenni bus was frequently packed to capacity, especially on Saturdays and during Fair Days; 'duplicates' were regularly required.

The early 1940s witnessed the introduction of diesel propulsion at Machynlleth, with the appearance of the efficient and popular KA series. The first to operate from Machynlleth was KA53, rostered to the Aberystwyth service. Others, which quickly found their way to the Corris–Aberllefenni, Dinas Mawddwy and Tywyn routes, were KA12 – one of the original fifteen which had a rear entry door – and KA55.

The attractive lines and proportions of post-war Bristol SLA 75 are evident as it operates a Dolgellau to Corris service down the pass towards Minffordd, c.1955. Later in its journey it would be faced with the prospect of negotiating the hairpin bend at Braich Goch Hotel.

GBJ Coll.

An undated trip, *c*.1950s, by Crosville staff at Machynlleth; destination unknown.
From the left, back row: Hugh Jones, Stan Jones, Idris Roderick, Ben Humphreys, Evan Williams, J. H. Humphreys, Mr Wynn ?, T. Alun Hughes, Albert …? Dick Holt, Edgar Davies, Alf Humphreys, Bill Davies, Llew Jones, J. W. Evans.
Front row: Dei Vaughan Owen, Geraint Jones, Percy Ward, John R. Jones, Stan Humphreys, Richie Holt, Penry Evans, Louis Morris, Jack Massa Edwards, Jimmy 'bach' Edwards, Will Edwards.

Courtesy Mrs Joan Brame.

Amongst the oddities which had somehow gravitated to Machynlleth was D3, which was unlike any other D-type. It was actually one of a pair, acquired second-hand from Leeds City Transport, although the second vehicle was never in service and only used for spare parts to keep D3 going. As purchased, D3 was a real city bus, having an open platform at the rear. Eventually, this was enclosed and fitted with sliding doors. Although not stylish, D3 was a popular and reliable vehicle, which possessed considerable charm.

The Crosville's method of tranferring buses to and from the works at Crane Wharf, Chester, must have varied throughout the system but, during the 1940–55 period at least, it was standard practice at Machynlleth to exchange one vehicle for another on Sundays, when there was no public service to consider. The vehicle to be exchanged would leave the depot, usually around 08.00 am. It was always interesting to work out later which of the local flock had been 'called home', achieved by peeping through the flap of the letter-box on the side door of the depot. Sometimes the exchange would be permanent, but usually a bus might reappear after several weeks, perhaps even in a change of livery, as during this period, when the LMS red was giving way to a new shade of green. Often, the attractiveness of the LMS colour was not fully appreciated at the time; frequently not until it had disappeared!

Throughout this period, D, E and F Leylands, new to the depot, were frequent visitors. They were the mainstay of the depot during 'petrol' days, but were generally unappreciated by enthusiasts and went unrecorded, save one, E63 notable for large and bold transfers of the number and company name. Amongst the final appearances of this type at Machynlleth were a pair which arrived at the railway station each weekday, about 08.00 am. Their passengers, from the villages north of Aberystwyth, would change to rail for the journey down the coast to work at the new military camps then being constructed at Tywyn, Tonfannau and further north. These buses were dedicated to this duty and languished all day on the depot forecourt, awaiting the evening's return trip; they did not mix with the local examples and none were recorded. An altogether more modern-looking vehicle of the later war-time era was T7; its elegant AEC radiator ensures it a place in the memory, as does the fact that it was the nearest the depot had to claiming a coach of its own in those days.

Without a doubt, the Crosville's numbering system fostered an interest in buses but, by the early 1950s, so many new vehicles were introduced that the system began to creak as it attempted to differentiate between the various sub-types. Nonetheless, it was gratifying to realize that as the good-looking Bristol-engined KB series arrived at Machynlleth, around 1950, they provided a tenuous link with the Bristol buses of the old railway, and also provide a fitting conclusion to this brief account which terminates here – although buses, admittedly under new ownership, continue to ply from the old Crosville depot, some 80 years later.

This image of Crosville's 1934-built garage at Machynlleth, appeared previously in *Great Western Corris* (p. 64) but is used again in preference to a more recent view as it displays the company name prominently. Coronation year, 1953.   *GBJ Coll.*

3. LLWYN-GWERN

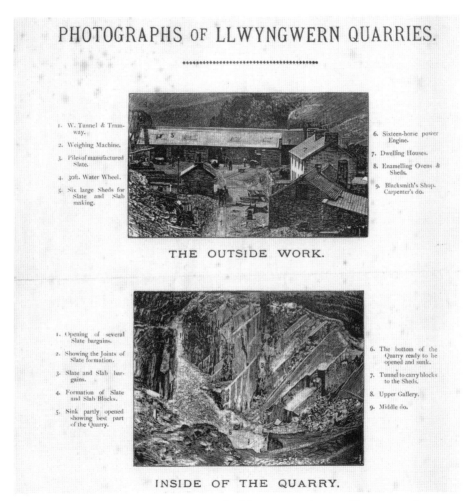

PHOTOGRAPHS OF LLWYNGWERN QUARRIES.

THE OUTSIDE WORK.

1. W. Tunnel & Tramway.
2. Weighing Machine.
3. Piles of manufactured Slate.
4. 30ft. Water Wheel.
5. Six large Sheds for Slate and Slab making.

6. Sixteen-horse power Engine.
7. Dwelling Houses.
8. Enamelling Ovens & Sheds.
9. Blacksmith's Shop. Carpenter's do.

INSIDE OF THE QUARRY.

1. Opening of several Slate bargains.
2. Showing the Joints of Slate formation.
3. Slate and Slab bargains.
4. Formation of Slate and Slab Blocks.
5. Sink partly opened showing best part of the Quarry.

6. The bottom of the Quarry ready to be opened and sunk.
7. Tunnel to carry blocks to the Sheds.
8. Upper Gallery.
9. Middle do.

The front cover of an undated Prospectus for Llwyn-gwern Quarry. These engravings were originally derived from early photographs which were not easily reproduced until the turn of the century, and consequently had to be hand-engraved on a metal plate. One wonders what became of the original photographs?

GBJ Coll.

35

Shades of yesteryear; a plain, early postcard, from the manager of the National Provincial bank of England, Machynlleth, 'begging to acknowledge receipt of your letter of today', dated May 15 [18]89 – what postal efficiency!

Private Collection.

Huw Briwnant Jones introduced W. E. Hayward to several people when he visited Machynlleth and Corris in 1941, in his quest for Corris Railway memorabilia and artefacts. This well-known print was amongst them. Hayward's comments are noted below.

The original of this photo was loaned to me by Mr Pritchard Jones of Corris, who drove the 1st Corris char-a-banc (B.T. & C.C. Ltd.) on the tours to Tal-y-llyn lake and Dolgelly. Date is most probably the late 1880s or early 1890 as the engine appears to be in the original condition with open back cab; note again the signalling and lower distant arm: wire fence has been replaced by a stone, or slate slab, wall. W. E. H. 26. 8. 1941.

GBJ Coll.

THE END OF A WELSH RAILWAY

A halt on the disused narrow-gauge rai'way between Corris and Machynlleth.

The narrow-gauge railway which for many years ran by the side of the road from Corris to Machynlleth, in the Dovey Valley, serving the slate quarries, is being demolished. British Railways decided to abandon their most Lilliputian acquisition when it was discovered that not only was it losing money but water was seeping under the line. Now the students of engines and rolling stock, as well as passengers who have used the line, will concern themselves about the fate of the two locomotives which drew wagons so tiny that if they became derailed they could be heaved back on to the line by hand. The stationmaster at Machynlleth says they will go to Swindon for scrap. Could not one of them, it might be asked, end its days in the Railway Museum?

Only one other line could provide them with work—the near-by Tal-y-llyn railway which runs a passenger service into the hills from Towyn during the summer months, and which has the same gauge of 2ft. 3in. But it does not want the Corris locomotives. The Tal-y-llyn line is privately owned, belonging to Sir Henry Haydn Jones, who was M.P. for Merioneth from 1910 to 1945. This celebrated little railway uses the same rolling stock that it began with 83 years ago.

Two locomotives.

37

It is possible that the Llwyn-gwern area can play a much more significant role in the prosperity of the present-day railway than occurred in former years; time will tell.

If the Centre for Alternative Technology and the railway can collaborate to create a strong visitor attraction and provide essential services, easily accessed by road-users, it would be welcomed and of enormous benefit to both parties.

As well as improving the railway itself, such developments would enhance the area further and increase the general facilities expected by holiday-makers. The congested station site at Corris was never perceived as the major site for the new railway, whose value to the locality has been completely reassessed in recent times. Experience elsewhere in north Wales has demonstrated that a revitalized railway could generate new interest and prosperity along the whole valley.

Consequently, this focus on Llwyn-gwern has resulted in a fresh appraisal of the humble photocopy (p. 37) which came to hand early in the 1950s. It was warmly received at the time but caused no great excitement. There was then little about Llwyn-gwern to set the pulses racing but today, as new images of the Corris have become increasingly difficult to discover, even humble photocopies are now often regarded with renewed interest. In truth, this particular example was neglected for many years and only commanded fresh attention in more recent times. This emphasized not only the strange publication date of the *Manchester Guardian* piece, but effectively recalled some of the doubt and uncertainty of that era, renewing the feeling that perhaps with a more favourable throw of the dice at that time, the Corris might have made it directly into preservation.

Nowadays, the 1886 landslip at Tan-y-coed is largely overlooked, despite the Corris Society's proposal to create a run-around loop near the site. Before the slip was repaired, it was photographed by McLardy, the Oswestry photographer, at the behest of George Owen, the engineer. The photograph survived until *c*.1960–70, when it disappeared in mysterious circumstances, although its absence was not discovered for some time. It is no exaggeration to state that this loss still haunts the writer.

This recent sketch is therefore based on an imperfect memory of maybe 55 years ago. Details are obviously sparse but certain features remain firm, particularly,

* the downward grade at this location and the suspended track, remembered as being in good order;
* the slip itself, 'decorated' by navvies dotted amongst the rubble, with interested spectators behind the slate fence.

The sepia print carried McLardy's imprint and was perhaps 8" x 10", but the size is uncertain. In essence, however, the sketch will bear comparison with the original composition, should it ever emerge.

GBJ

This twenty-first century view of the site of the slip is rendered vague and unclear by shade, moss and foliage. Regrettably, it was not possible at the time to see whether a date stone had been built into the new wall. Perhaps one may yet emerge, one day. 30 May 2002.

GBJ

When Neville Fields visited Corris during the mid-1940s, this composition emerged as one of the more unusual. The reason for the unorthodox 'stop' is not apparent – it may have been related to the bicycles in the quarry waggons or to a nut-picking session. Mr Campbell Thomas occasionally forsook his formal 'main line' Station Master's livery for the weekly Corris inspection.

Neville Fields/GBJ Coll.

Quite obviously, preservation was never considered in 1949. What has later become the quite astounding story of the renewed Corris Railway was not even dreamt of at that time. Progress since 1966 however, although often seeming slow to the impatient, has been most remarkable.

Amongst the major achievements to date, are

- the reopening of the line to passengers between Corris and Maes-poeth,;
- the construction of the No. 4 'look-alike';
- an excellent start on the construction of the new carriages, two to date, and the most vital shed in which to store them away from the worst of the weather;
- also the launch of a fund, which continues to increase, to build a No. 3 'look-alike'.

Members are ready and anxious to take another major step forward, advancing the track southward towards the Llwyn-gwern/Machynlleth area. Future developments in this part of the Dulas valley are anticipated most keenly. Opportunities for Corris progress abound.

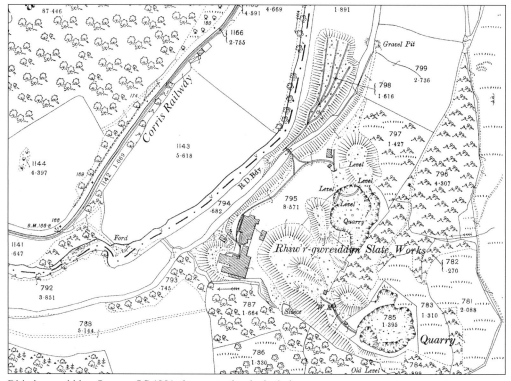

Rhiw'r-gwreiddyn Quarry. OS 1901, demonstrating its isolation.   *NLW.*

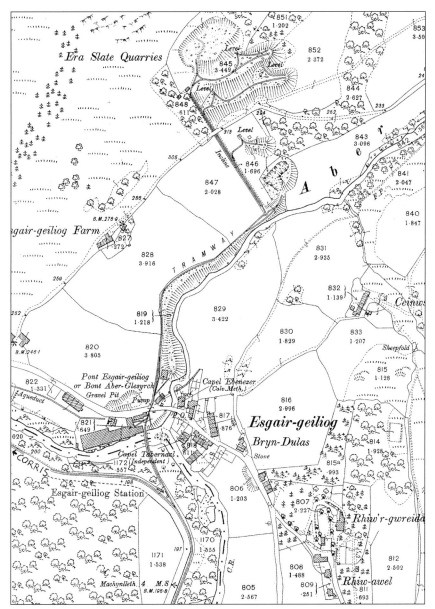

The Era Quarry, Esgairgeiliog. OS 1901.

The 1901 Ordnance Survey maps of the three main quarries of the lower Dulas valley are included here as they rarely command as much attention as the larger quarries elsewhere in the valley. No attempt is made to furnish any account of their histories, but anyone seeking such information is recommended to refer to *Slate Quarrying at Corris* by Alun John Richards, Gwasg Carreg Gwalch, 1994.

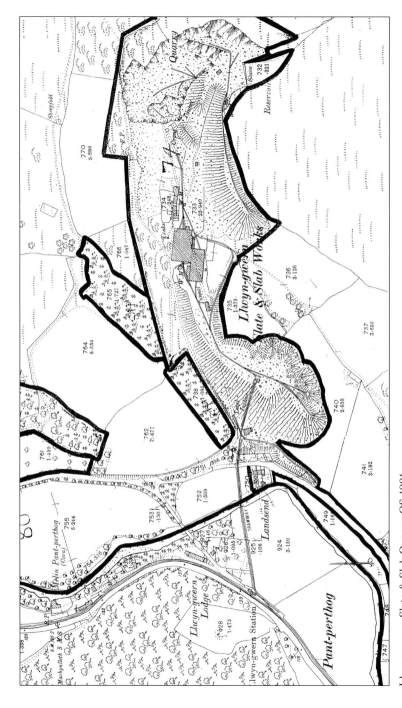

Llwyn-gwern Slate & Slab Quarry. OS 1901.
No explanation can be offered for the heavy black lines.

NLW.

42

4. FINAL FRAGMENTS

The following snippets of the Corris story have no claim for a more prominent place elsewhere, but are here listed as:

    i)   Horse operation;
    ii)   Culture and leisure;
    iii)   Trip on the Tal-y-llyn, *c.*1946;
    iv)   The Lamp;
    v)   The final photographic trawl.

i) Horse Operation

Generally, on the Corris, horses only drew attention to themselves if they mis-behaved, fell sick or lame, or were involved in accidents. During independent days and before the coming of the internal combustion engine, the Corris laid great store on horses and reports to the Board in those days, during the Dix and O'Sullivan eras, made continual references to the constant buying and selling of stock according to seasonal demands and the variable fitness of individual animals – the lame and the sick were 'moved on' whenever possible. It is fairly reasonable to assume that not all incidents were reported to the Board, particularly minor ones, but after the internal combustion engine established itself, the number of horses was reduced dramatically until, by the later GW years, the solitary horse stabled at Corris covered

David/Dafydd Roberts alongside one of the GW horses, at an unknown location. Precisely how many Great Western horses worked the Corris between 1930 and closure in the early 1950s is not known. There must surely have been many instances when a horse could not continue and had to be replaced. How this was achieved is not currently well-known. Undated.

Corris Railway Society.

the area from Esgairgeiliog to Top Corris and Aberllefenni, including the Ratgoed branch. Only for a period during the Second World War was another railway horse active in the area, when the solitary delivery lorry (an old flat-fronted Thornycroft) working from the goods warehouse at Machynlleth was replaced by a horse, stabled in the better of the two Corris stables in the Corris yard at Machynlleth.

David Roberts was thus the Great Western's last horse-shunter on the Corris, and a familiar figure around the area as he worked the horse mainly between Corris and Aberllefenni, on his way between the stables and the quarries – the equivalent of a kind of 'light-engine' movement!

The last Corris Railway horse-shunter at Machynlleth was John Jones, who retired in 1930, aged 73, having served the Corris for over 50 years – the last 30 with the same horse. This remarkable record brought him to the notice of the local press which ensured that the photograph below appeared in the *County Times* in May 1930.

Interestingly, the first two waggons represent a type of bolster waggon introduced around the time of the First World War; they rarely feature in photographs and were quickly scrapped by the GWR in the early 1930s. The photograph also reveals the coupling/harness arrangements which minimised injury to the horse, in the event of an 'over-run' for example. Other duties at Machynlleth also included the periodic removal of narrow-gauge waggons via a special stub-point, which enabled the horse to transfer them to different areas of the standard-gauge yard to facilitate the transfer of goods. The stub-point survives.

ii) Culture and Leisure

This brief list records randomly a few events which took full advantage of the services of the Corris Railway during the final years of passenger operation; it constitutes the nearest we have to an official railway diary. It also demonstrates clearly the contribution of the railway to the life of the Dulas valley community. Similar events had obviously featured prominently on the railway from its earliest days, but no record of them seems to have survived, apart from official references which featured from time to time in official minutes to the Directors.

1927 February	8	2 loads coal off rails 11.25 Up train. 12.20 down only to Lliwdy. Bus to Lliwdy & back* *From Machynlleth.
March	26	Carnarvon [*sic*] Band Festival – Wolverhampton Football.
April	6	Engine pulling poorly 11.25 & 3.45.
	15	Good Friday – All services suspended.
	18	Spl train 8.30 pm xCorris. 9.00 xMCH for Aberllefenni, returning to Corris only.
	25	Spl to Aberllefenni @ 9.15 Missionary Exhibition @ Machynlleth.
	29	Spl to Aberllefenni @ 9.30 & 11.15
	30	" " " "
May	16	Fair @ MCH 5.25 Up running to Aberllefenni, Also Spl @ 10.00 pm
	21	Band Contest @ MCH. 8.30 to MCH 9.15 ex MCH
	23	Graig Chapel Festival (7.30 held till 8.00 pm)
June	6	Whit Monday Singing @ Aberdyfi. Spl Up 9.15.
	9	Wesleyan Assembly @ Machynlleth 8.30 Up exMCH through to Aberllefenni.
June	16	Maen-gwyn Singing Festival. 8.20 to Aberllefenni.
	24	Dovey Flooded but all trains as usual.
July	23	Corris Slate Trip to Aberystwyth. Both engines.
August	1	Bank Holiday. Up Spl @ 9.15 for Aberllefenni.
	6	Band Contest @ Holyhead. Corris Band competing. 11.0 pm Up for Corris and Aberllefenni.
	20	Show, Sports & Eisteddfod @ Corris. Late Spl 9.20 pm to Corris & Aberllefenni.
September	10	Sports at Corris.
	19	Fair at Machynlleth. Late 9.0 Up for Corris and Aberllefenni.

iii) Trip on the Tal-y-llyn c.1946

In 1946, the writer knew little about the Tal-y-llyn. Occasional visits to friends in Tywyn were not informative, nor had there been any encouraging sightings of a train of any kind at Wharf. Nothing was ever glimpsed as the GW service entered Tywyn *en route* from Machynlleth, save one or two empty slate waggons and some neat, very stationary, stacks of slates; nothing stirred. Later, on enquiring, it became apparent that the rolling-stock was not kept at Wharf but up the line, at Pen-dre. Here also, during those dark days, visits were not particularly rewarding; only glimpses of rolling-stock could be discerned through unclear windows or through chinks in the slatted carriage shed. Again, no movement was apparent, nor was there any public timetable to suggest that things did indeed move occasionally.

Gradually, however, it was learned that trains ran only on certain days, more or less as required. It became a matter of enquiring, a task finally achieved through the kindness of a booking-clerk at Machynlleth who, in due course, duly arranged a visit. Photography in those days was not feasible; illustrations used here date from the 1950s. Regrettably, the date was not seen to be that important at the time, so it was not recorded, but it was certainly during the 'independent' days of Sir Henry Haydn Jones, around 1946.

Before setting out from Machynlleth, it was deemed prudent to take the precaution of ringing up the Wharf station, to make sure a service was indeed operating that day. John Pugh, a fellow enthusiast, came along for the experience, and when we presented ourselves at Wharf, a person we later discovered to be the redoubtable Mr Edward Thomas sold us the tickets and, in due course, offered a choice of seats, either in one of the 4-wheel carriages or in one of the empty slate waggons returning to Bryneglwys Quarry. With little hesitation, we opted for the novelty of travel in a slate waggon. As far as can be recalled, there were about three empty waggons that day but we were the only ones, amongst a small number of passengers, who elected to travel alfresco. When we expressed our preference, we were directed to a waggon which had been fitted with two primitive 'seats' – sturdy, but slightly warped pieces of elm, which had been slotted between the bars of the waggon, with about 4–5 inches protruding outside the loading-gauge, assuming there was one. There was no fixture of any kind. Such a ploy was feasible with the 'cotton-reel' or bobbin-spaced bar waggons which still operated on the Tal-y-llyn. Similar waggons had all disappeared from the Corris, when the Braich-goch Quarry transferred their slates to road transport (actually a steam lorry) in 1926, although a number of surviving waggons could still be seen in the yard at Braich-goch at this time. One or two of these may have been used internally, but most were derelict.

The most notable feature of this journey, however, was the deplorable condition of the track. Each rail joint betwen Tywyn and Abergynolwyn was badly 'dipped', emphasising the complete absence of any form of springing on the waggons, as they climbed up and down from one rail-end to the next. Variations in gauge were another matter. The cynical could claim that each rail left Wharf station at a slightly different angle to its near companion; the wonder was that both seemed to keep in touch with each other most of the way to

At the end of a working day in August 1957, former Corris No. 3 reversed the empty carriage stock up the gradient from Wharf, towards Pen-dre, past the plinthed Welsh Highland 2–6–2T *Russell*, offered a refuge at Wharf whilst awaiting restoration.

GBJ

Abergynolwyn. The Corris, in comparison, provided a 'glide-ride' – by the end of the journey, we were well-qualified to pass judgement!

Amongst other distinctive impressions of the day which still survive, rather surprisingly perhaps, are memories of the floor of our waggon. This was covered, as might well be expected, perhaps, in fine dust and small chips of slate, from stacking and rubbing on the journey from Bryneglwys, but what made the biggest and most unexpected impression were the pieces of fern and other vegetation, which had been snagged from the prolific and dense lineside undergrowth. After the slates had been transferred to main line waggons at Wharf, fragments of fern remained and became intermingled with the slate chips and dust on the floor; they still provide a poignant reminder of that day.

The return journey, needless to say, was spent 'inside', on the cushions. The ride was a slight improvement on the 'up' journey but the carriages still had to negotiate each rail-end although, undeniably, the cushions helped. The locomotive was *Dolgoch*. It all amounted to a unique experience.

The Tal-y-llyn's No. 1 being checked at Rhydyronen, during its maiden run after an important re-build in 1958. It was returned to Tywyn from Gibbons' Brothers works in the west midlands on Saturday 14 June, and promptly appeared on trial, without delay, the following day.

The figure who had popped his head into the engine's cab was Lord Northesk, a keen supporter of the Tal-y-llyn at that time.

Hugh Jones, a driver on the TR, lived nearby and had obviously used ex Corris No. 4 for his transport home the previous evening, for it was parked thoughtfully, out of the way, on the adjacent grass-grown siding. 15 June 1958.

GBJ

iv) The Lamp

Although the writer has known this little tale for most of his life, it eluded his attention completely during compilation of *Tales of the Old Corris* in 2008 and was only restored to the memory when attention was drawn to it later by Meinir Coleman. Fortunately, Meinir had also heard the story from the writer's mother.

Absence of any form of official information prevents a formal verification of the facts, but there is no reason to doubt the veracity of the salient features. The story is undated, but may well belong to the period either just before or during the Great War. At that time, the engineman of the early morning shift was visited by a 'knocker-up' or 'caller-up' whose task, after he had raised steam in the engine, was to confirm that the driver was up and about. On this occasion, it seems that the last person to bed in the Roberts' household the previous evening had neglected to turn off the light on the oil lamp, which had remained lit all night. Thus, when the cleaner arrived sometime during the small hours, a light was visible through the drawn curtains and the cleaner, assuming that William Roberts was about, did not trouble to knock the door but turned and made his way back to the shed.

Later in the morning, there was obviously great consternation. The consequences were not noted, although it may safely be assumed that those who had a hand in the error would have been well aware that they made quite a name for themselves that day! It is also safe to assume that they would have had no inkling that their misdemeanour would be a topic for discussion in 2015.

Perhaps the most surprising aspect of the account centres on the fact that the little Corris Railway employed a practice more generally utilised by main line rather than narrow-gauge companies. One wonders how many other Welsh narrow-gauge companies – with the possible exception of the Ffestiniog perhaps – would have employed a fitter and/or cleaner on night duty? We will never know for certain.

CORRIS RAILWAY.

MAIN LINE.

WORKING TIME TABLE for month of OCTOBER, 1908, and until further notice.

DOWN.

Station	1 G. & P. a.m.	3 mixed a.m. (C)	5 Pass a.m.	7 Pass a.m.	9 Pass a.m.	11 Pass a.m.	13 Pass p.m.	15 Pass p.m.	17 Pass p.m.	19 mixed p.m.	21 Pass p.m.	23 Pass p.m.	25 Goods p.m. (S)	Miles from Aberllefeni
Aberllefeni dep.			7M45			10 0	12 35			3 35			8 0	
Mathews Mill Siding ,,														
Fronwen Siding ,,			sig			sig	sig			sig			sig	
Garneddwen {arr.			7M53			10 8	12 43			3 43			8 20	1
Garneddwen {dep.			8 0			10 10	12 45			3 55				
Corris {arr.							12 52							1½
Corris {dep.		5 35	8 7			sig	12 59	2 10		4 2		5 35		
Maespoeth Junction {dep.		5 40												2
Evans' Bridge ,,		5 46						2 17				5 42		3
Esgairgeiliog ,,		5 58	8 14			sig		2 24		4 9		5 49		4
Llwyngwern ,,		sig	sig			sig	sig	sig		sig		sig		
Ffridd Gate ,,														6
Machynlleth arr.		6 15	8 25			10 35	1 10	2 35		4 20		6 0		6½

UP.

Station	2 Engine a.m. (Q)	4 mixed a.m.	6 Goods a.m.	8 Pass a.m.	10 Pass a.m.	12 Pass a.m.	14 Pass p.m.	16 G. & P. p.m.	18 Pass p.m.	20 Pass p.m.	22 Pass p.m.	24 Pass p.m.	26 Pass p.m.	Miles from Machynlleth
Machynlleth dep.		6 30	9 5			11 30	1 35	2 45		5 0		7 20		
Ffridd Gate ,,		sig	sig			sig	sig	sig		sig		sig		1
Llwyngwern ,,		6 42	9 17			11 42	1 47	2 57		5 12		7 32		
Esgairgeiliog ,,		6 48	9 23			11 48	1 53	3 3		5 18		7 38		3
Evans' Bridge ,,		sig	sig			sig		sig						4
Maespoeth Junction {arr. {dep.	5 20	6 55	9 30			11 55		3 10						
Corris {arr.	5 25						2 0			5 25		7 45		5
Corris {dep.		6M57	9 32			11 57		3 12				7s47		
Garneddwen ,,		sig	sig			sig		sig				sig		6
Fronwen Siding ,,														
Mathews Mill Siding ,,														
Aberllefeni arr.		7M 5	9 40			12 5		3 20				7s55		6½

sig—Stop if required.   M—Mondays only.   C—Carriages attached to this train from Corris on Mondays only.   Q—Trains marked "Q" only run when required.   S—Mondays, Wednesdays, and Saturdays only.

Guards, Station Masters, and Porters must see that Passengers are not allowed to use the seats in the gangways.

This 1908–09 copy of a Corris Railway Working Timetable, thought to approximate to the era of the tale of the lamp, illustrates the need for a 'knocker-up' at this time. His first task must have been to raise steam for the engine to be ready to leave the shed by 05.20 and depart Corris fifteen minutes later.   *GBJ Coll.*

v) The Final Photographic Trawl

This choice is governed not so much by subject matter but by what remains unused or under-used hitherto. The selection may lack cohesion, but an attempt has been made to place the images in a chronological order.

This 1909 view along the 'up' platform of the Cambrian station at Machynlleth, is part of a larger well-known composition but, selective enlargement emphasises, hopefully, the sign used to guide passengers who had arrived from coastal resorts and who sought the narrow-gauge trains for Corris. They were directed initially down a substantial and rather formidable flight of steps, to the lower goods yard.

The Locomotive Club of Great Britain/GBJ Coll.

The Corris station (termed 'Low Level' by the GWR) lay across this goods yard, where a narrow-gauge train would invariably await. On this occasion No. 3 was on duty, just a matter of months before final closure. 1930.

Courtesy of E. A. Gurney-Smith. GBJ Coll.

When Huw Briwnant Jones returned from service in France in 1919, he forsook his previous employment in London for work on the Corris Railway where, by 1921, he was a passenger guard. He posed with his sister (extreme left) and other family members in September 1921.

GBJ Coll.

The contemporary fingerprints indicate an amateur's handiwork, but this small stained 2 x 1 print is the only surviving close-up of Driver William Roberts on the footplate of No. 2 at Machynlleth; undated but *c.*1922.

GBJ Coll.

A fine view in the George & Son, Real Photograph Series, perhaps dating from the early 1920s. This particular example, with a message in Welsh, was sent by the new maid at Chapel House, (*lower r/h corner*) to her friends in Llangaffo, Anglesey. The card was posted and franked at Corris on 18 August 1927. The Ratgoed Tramway may be seen crossing the fields in the middle distance, running past the village school.

GBJ Coll.

This is one of the views shown to W. E. Hayward and copied by him in 1941. This copy, however, is taken from an original print. Corris *c.*1920.

Anon. GBJ Coll.

An early view of No. 4, soon after the take-over by the GWR. Note well flattened ground and absence of weeds around the runing lines – perhaps due to constant use by buses; also, the engine's number-plate in original maker's condition displaying No. 4047, and the absence of any sign of ownership on the side of the waggon. *c*.1931. *LGRP/GBJ Coll.*

No. 3 'dead' at Maes-poeth, but with firewood in the cab, ready to light-up. *c*.1945–47.

P. Q. Treloar/GBJ Coll.

This blemished print of a scene within the shed at Maes-poeth, *c*.1938, shows No. 4 being prepared for the day's work and No. 3 being rested.

S. H. P. Higgins Collection, NRM.

Trapped on the 'Braich'. Volunteers pause in their endeavours to release a car trapped in snow *c*.1938. Apart from five names, no further information is available. It could be that the Crosville bus, the RAC motor bike and side-car, and the postman's van were all left at the Braich Goch Hotel, after the struggle through the snow from Machynlleth. It was obviously easier to reach the stricken car from that point, rather than battling up the more direct but slippery and treacherous slope from the village.

The five who have been identified were, from the left: Ted Blayney, bus driver; unknown; Will Arnold, RAC Roadside Patrolman; Alun Hughes, bus conductor; the car owner (perhaps not from the area); Norman Leeke, postman from Machynlleth; PC Tom Lloyd Williams.

Courtesy of the late Dei Vaughan Owen/GBJ Coll.

This harsh photocopy seems to be all that survives of what was, basically, a fine portrayal of the Corris triumvirate, Driver Humphreys, Lengthman Teddy Jones and Guard Robert Price Owen. The source of the original is not known, but *c*.1947.

GBJ Coll.

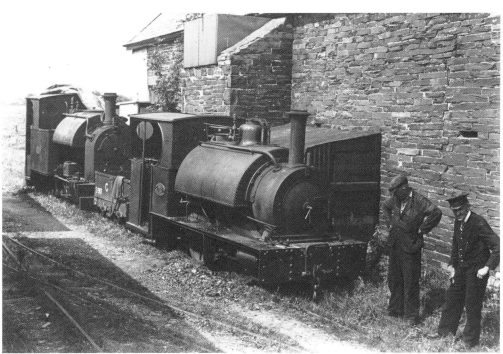

A photograph which reflects all the poignancy and saddness of the final months; Humphrey and Price Owen captured in pensive mood by Stanhope Baker, 30 July 1948.

GBJ Coll.

Corris Caravan Park, located across the valley from Pont Ifans/Maes-poeth, has proved a convenient refuge for caravaners over the years. *c.*1955.

GBJ Coll.

The approach to Corris *c.*1960, looking along the A487, with the path of the erstwhile horse tramway to the Upper Corris quarries still discernable alongside. The Vale of Aberllefenni lies directly ahead, whilst Fronfelen Hall may be seen across the valley.

Photo Precision Cards/GBJ Coll.

This grass-grown causeway at Aberllefenni carried the horse tramway to the Ratgoed and Cymerau Quarries, across the Aberllefenni Quarry reservoir. Photographed in 1965.

G. H. Platt/courtesy W. G. Rear/GBJ Coll.

Also at Aberllefenni, the lightly-laid tramway track and narrow roadway leading from the quarry mill, up the Hengae valley, to the Aberllefenni Quarry itself. 1965. *G. H. Platt/courtesy W.G. Rear/GBJ Coll.*

Former Corris Railway employees, with wives or husbands, were proud to assemble outside the refurbished museum/refreshment block, during a group visit.

Richard Greenhough.

Corris station. This was the initial refurbishment by the society, which has served the revitalised railway for more than a decade, but will shortly make way for an improved layout. Present plans are for the green portakabin to be relocated and the platform surface bricks (originally from Tywyn promenade) to be redeployed in a new configuration. Photograph 30 March 2001.

GBJ

On 1 April 2009, a celebratory gravity train was run, 150 years after the original event. It is seen here rounding the curve near Maes-y-llan, as it left Corris.

GBJ

Further along the route, on the same run, it was photographed again as it approached Maes-poeth. Although lacking the amount of rolling-stock available for gravity workings, as on the Ffestiniog for example, the Corris is still proud that it can replicate the working practice of a century and a half ago.

GBJ

These two photographs have appeared in print previously, but not on the same occasion. They are brought together here to entertain the theory that they may, just possibly, be connected and were perhaps taken on the same occasion?

Could the upper photograph by Roger Kidner, showing No. 4 having just crossed the river Dyfi, also have captured the photographer who recorded the end view of the van? A shadowy figure stands alongside the right-hand side of the van in Roger Kidner's photograph; was this perchance H. B. Tours ?

The figure approachng the gate, recorded in H. B. Tours photograph of the van (*below*), is believed to have been Roger Kidner, returning to base, having duly completed his photography at that location.

Kidner and Tours are known to have visited the Corris together in 1939. It rained!

Roger Kidner and H. B. Tours/GBJ Coll.

ADDENDUM

This brief appendage was not part of the original plan but the idea emerged when the first set of proofs returned from the publisher, and a few blank pages at the end (of the book) seemed to offer an opportunity to provide an interesting contrast by presenting some of the latest projects on the railway.

The few photographs inserted here – all courtesy of the Corris Railway Society – cannot, just within a page or two, adequately reflect the variety and intensity of the work undertaken by volunteers, much of which is often low-profile or administrative work behind the scenes. What follows can be no more than a very brief sketch of the Corris in 2015.

The Impossible Dream* – No. 7 and two Maes-poeth carriages. Early Septenber 2015.

*(with acknowledgements to *The Man from la Mancha*.)

Infrastructure

Before further track can be laid to a new southern terminus, attention has been focussed on the current layout at Corris, which is severely restricted by the very cramped location.

To this end, interested members led primarily by Paul Bailey, are striving towards a solution, but much administrative work is necessary before real progress can be seen on the ground. Students at the City of Glasgow College, as part of their coursework, have contributed a scale model of the Corris site, which will prove useful for publicity and invaluable during further discussions with the various interested bodies. Furthermore, intermediate locations such as the projected level-crossing at the junction of the minor road from Esgairgeiliog and the A487 trunk road, for example, will require careful planning and consideration by Her Majesty's Railway Inspectorate (HMRI), as will any development of the old station site at Esgairgeiliog itself.

Hitherto, no plans have been published regarding the southern end of the projected extension to Llwyngwern, but surveys have been conducted with the approval of the landowners concerned. Hopefully, such a development could embrace the nearby Centre for Advanced Technology (CAT). At least two alternative routes could be considered by planning and highway authorities – a time-consuming process perhaps – but it is underway.

Rolling Stock

Progress on the rolling stock front however, appears more positive, and certainly more apparent.

Corris locomotives Nos 3 and 4 still exist of course, but have been well established on the nearby Talyllyn Railway since the early 1950s. Nowadays, they only return to the Corris very occasionally, as special visitors. Consequently, the decision had to be taken to build anew. Plans for a new version of No. 4 came to fruition on the Corris in 2005, as No. 7, and it has proved popular and generally reliable: continuous fettling over the past ten years or so has effectively 'fine-tuned' its performance.

Obtaining plans for a replica No. 3 was not such a straightforward process, as the original drawings no longer exist. With the Talyllyn's blessing, however, the original No. 3 has been meticulously and skilfully measured and a new set of drawings produced, enabling a positive start to be made on preparations for construction. Thus far, the boiler and main-frame, together with several castings and fittings have been produced and placed in store until sufficient finance has been accumulated, when final assembly can commence at the workshops of Alan Keef Ltd, near Ross-on-Wye. It will become Corris No. 10.

In early 2015, most members were somewhat taken by surprise when a chunky, modern diesel locomotive, by Orenstein & Koppel, was purchased privately by two members and presented to the railway. Numbered 11, this will provide an instant reserve of power for

No. 7 at Maes-poeth, at the commencement of its ten-yearly boiler examination, when it was dismantled, examined and re-built over winter months; a fine achievement.

The boiler and fire-box removed from the frames…

…which were taken outside, to create more working-space.

An early stage in the proceedings.

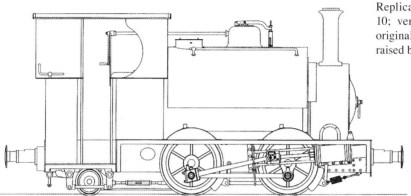

Projected Corris No. 3 Replica, to run as No. 10; very similar to the original, but with cab roof raised by 4¼".

An impressive front view of No. 11.

New No. 11 seems anxious to acquaint itself with the route to Corris.

New carriage No. 22, resplendent at Maes-poeth, before being unveiled. Early September 2015.

Work continues on the steel frame of carriage 23, mostly during weekends, but with help from the 'Tuesday Gang'. Note the excellent facilities.

emergencies, or it can be pressed into action during periods when passenger numbers are lighter and do not warrant raising steam. It seems likely to prove an attractive asset .

As far as carriages are concerned, the society has every right to be extremely proud of the achievements of the small, dedicated and skilful carriage-building group. Materials for four carriages have been generously provided by member Mike Cruttenden, and two carriages, to the original and unique Corris pattern, have already been built at Maes-poeth. Using modern methods of construction, work is also progressing well on the production of a second pair of carriages. Construction and eventual storage of these is within the excellent carriage shed provided by the society (2009).

Considering the comparatively late formation of the society (1966) and the modest number of society members, these achievements represent unbelievable progress, particularly to anyone who can recall the closure of the old railway in 1948.

Meanwhile, plans have been prepared to re-lay the track south from Maes-poeth, when circumstances permit; some track panels have already been purchased and are held in secure storage. Signs of progress are most encouraging but despite evidence of judicious planning, there is always need of further funding – and volunteers to accelerate the work.

Are you interested? Can you help ?

The story of the Corris continues…

Mechanised ballast-loading on the Corris.   *Courtesy of local contractor Richard Evans 'Y Rugog'.*

A general view of the southern end of the layout at Maes-poeth showing, behind the stop-block, the path to be taken when the line is extended towards Tan-y-coed and Llwyn-gwern. The route of the original alignment south at this point is visible on the right-hand side. This is now a head-shunt to the ballast-loading siding. The severe double-bend over Nant y Goedwig of the old route hereabouts has been eliminated by the new alignment.